Noisy Frog

Sing-Along

By John Himmelman

DAWN PUBLICATIONS

For Sage — JH

Library of Congress Cataloging-in-Publication Data
Himmelman, John.
 Noisy frog sing-along / by John Himmelman. -- First edition.
   pages cm
 Summary: "Listen closely to the sounds, often very loud, that frogs make
without ever opening their mouths. Together they make a concert! Endnotes
present facts and activities about these lively and fascinating
creatures"--Provided by publisher.
 Audience: Ages 3 to 8.
 ISBN 978-1-58469-339-0 (hardback) -- ISBN 978-1-58469-340-6 (pbk.) 1.
Frog sounds--Juvenile literature. 2. Toad sounds--Juvenile literature. I.
Title.
 QL668.E2H563 2013
 597.8'91594--dc23

                        2013009691

Book design and production by Patty Arnold, Menagerie Design & Publishing

Manufactured by Regent Publishing Services, Hong Kong
Printed July, 2013, in ShenZhen, Guangdong, China

10 9 8 7 6 5 4 3 2 1
First Edition

Dawn Publications
12402 Bitney Springs Road
Nevada City, CA 95959
530-274-7775
nature@dawnpub.com

Frogs sing when they get together. Just the males sing - they want to be heard by the females! They fill their big, bulgy throat pouches with air, and sing out. Some males are high and squeaky. Some are deep and rumbly. Others are very LOUD. And they sing without ever opening their mouths!

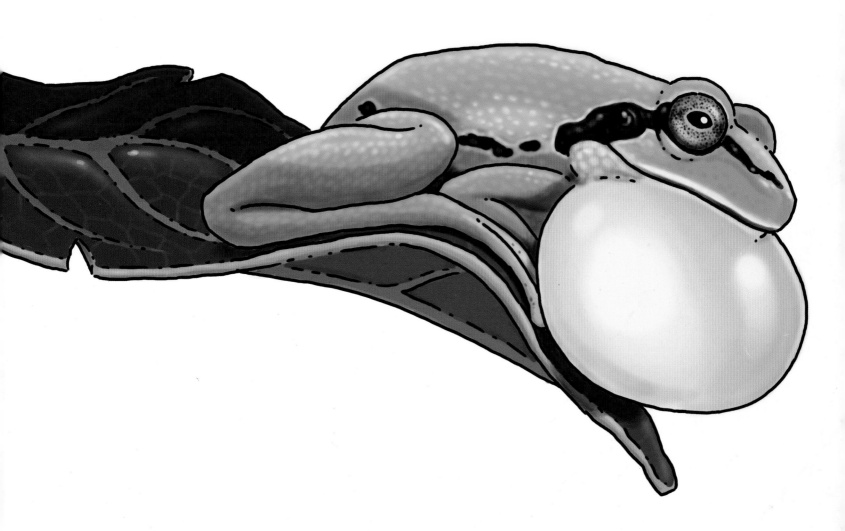

A Peeper peeps in the cold spring rain.

peep - peep - peep

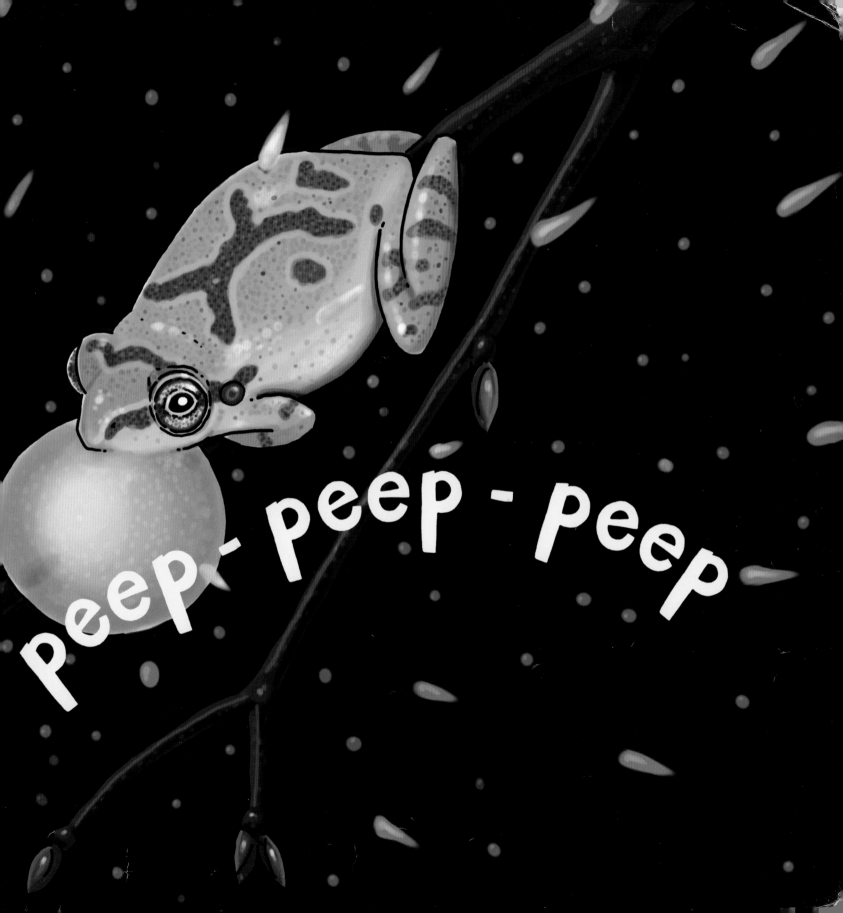

peep - peep - peep

Green Frogs plunk like banjos

at the edge of a pond.

PLUNK.

PLUNK.

PLUNK

Green Frog

Some Toads trill sweetly in the garden.
Toads are a type of frog.

Some **Toads** growl in the sand like angry sheep.

Fowlers Toad

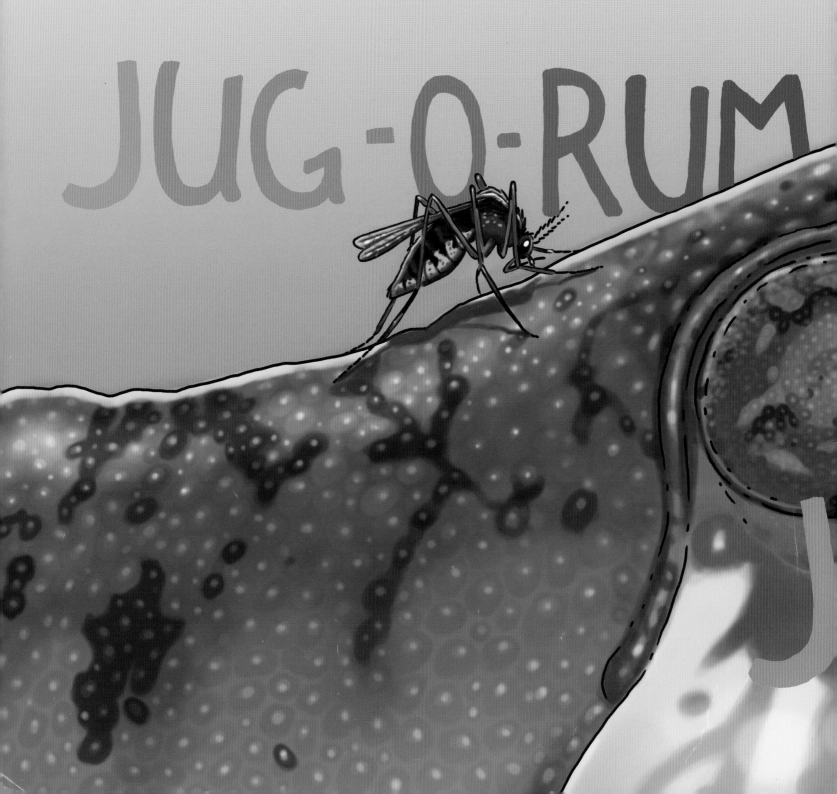

The great big **Bullfrog** JUG-O-RUMS

JUG-O-RUM

A Pickerel Frog growls deeply while floating on water.

ROOOWL

These Chorus Frogs are creaking in a creek.

A **Mink Frog** cuks in a chilly pond.

visór

CUK CUK CU

CU

A close relative to frogs, this Salamander crawls
by silently in the wet leaves.
He doesn't have a throat pouch to sing with.

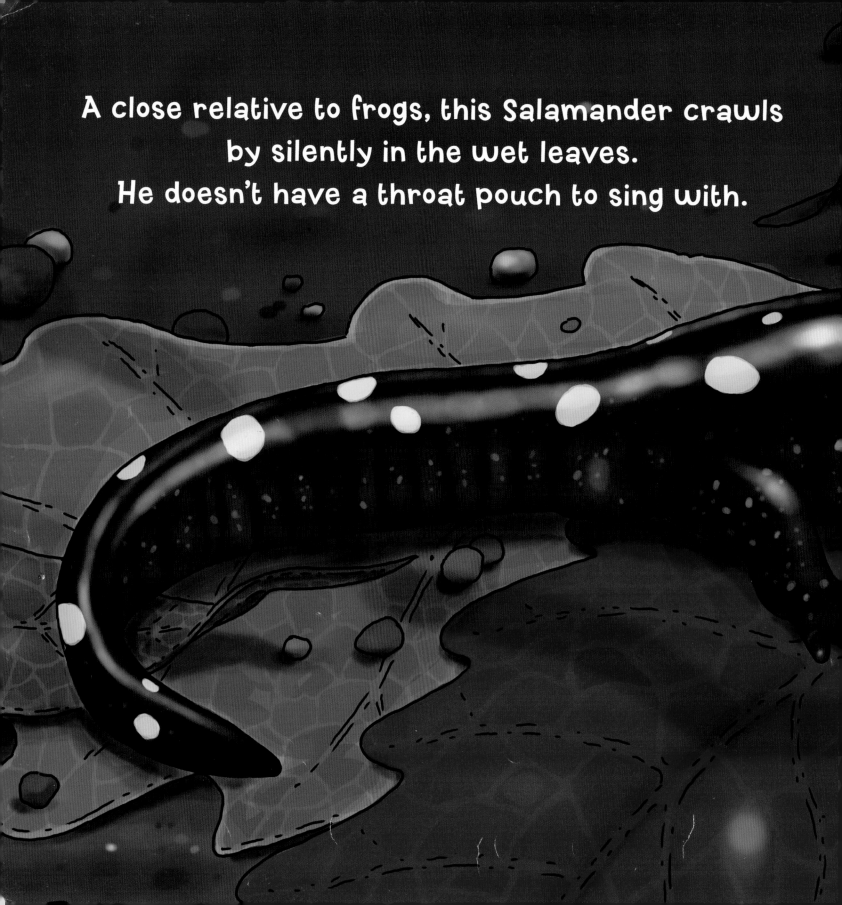

after it rains in the desert.

Some Tree Frogs go ribbit in the morning fog.

ribbit

ribbit ribbit

meep meep

Some Tree Frogs meep on skinny branches.

Gather all the frogs together and hear them sing!

ROOOWL ribbit

PLUNK....

creeeak PLUNK... ROOOWL

eak

PLUNK... CUK CUK

AAA JUG-O-RUM

RAAAAAAA

CUK

bit Breeeeeeeeeee

About the Noisy Frogs

Spring Peepers call from low branches at the edges of ponds throughout the eastern half of the United States and Canada. Sometimes you will find them crawling on your windows. They are hunting the insects attracted to the lights in your house.

Green Frogs are very common in ponds and lakes in the eastern half of the United States and Canada. They spend most of their lives in water. In winter they bury themselves in the mud at the bottom and survive by breathing through their skin.

American Toads are frogs that spend most of their adult life outside of the water. They have very bumpy skin and a poison gland behind each eye. This makes them very distasteful to skunks, raccoons, and other mammals that eat frogs.

Fowler's Toads gather in fresh water springs and rain puddles. They are one of the few frogs you can find on an ocean beach, but they stay away from the salt water, which dries out their skin. They are named after the naturalist who first found them in Massachusetts in the 1800's.

American Bullfrogs are North America's largest frog. They are found all over the United States although they are native only to the eastern half of the country, and are considered an invasive species elsewhere. If you order frogs legs in a restaurant, they will have been supplied by this species. Their deep call in spring and summer can be felt as a rumble in your chest!

Pickerel Frogs are eastern amphibians that are often confused with Leopard Frogs. Pickerel Frogs have rectangular spots, compared with Leopard Frog's more circular spots. Pickerel Frogs have bright orange coloring under the legs. This warns hungry mammals that they will not taste good.

Western Chorus Frogs live in a large area from Canada to the Gulf of Mexico, and from New Jersey to Arizona. They are easiest found on warm nights when the males are calling for females. Many males call together—in a chorus—which helps the females hear them up to a half a mile away!

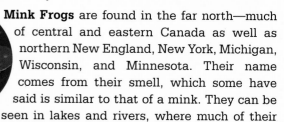

Mink Frogs are found in the far north—much of central and eastern Canada as well as northern New England, New York, Michigan, Wisconsin, and Minnesota. Their name comes from their smell, which some have said is similar to that of a mink. They can be seen in lakes and rivers, where much of their time is spent resting on lily pads.

Spotted Salamanders are not frogs, but like frogs they spend their immature stage as larvae that live and breathe underwater. Larvae are the salamander version of tadpoles. Spotted Salamanders spent most of their lives underneath logs and beneath leaves on the ground. They only return to the water to breed and lay eggs.

Couch's Spadefoots live in deserts and other dry, sandy habitats in the southwest. Much of their life is spent beneath the sand. When the rains come, they come to the surface and gather in the puddles. Their hind foot has a special spade-like tool for digging their way back into the sand when their habitat dries out.

Pacific Treefrogs make the sound most people think of when asked what sound a frog makes—"ribbit". While they can be found, day and night, clinging to branches with their large toe pads, these frogs are most often found on the ground among the shrubs at the edge of ponds.

Green Treefrogs are great climbers, and would rather climb a branch than hop away from danger. Their green color helps them stay hidden in the surrounding leaves. They live in the southern United States all the way from Maryland to Texas. Many of them are kept as pets.

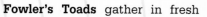